Dedicated to my parents:
Constant Georges MERITZA
(1929-2011)
Josiane MERITZA
(1936-)
and to the one who shares my life
my partner Sophie

<u>Special thanks :</u>

Yoann MERITZA

OPEN
THIS
LAST
DOOR

Éditeur:

BoD-Books on Demand,

12/14 rond point des Champs Élysées

75008 Paris, France

*Printing: BoD-Books on Demand, Norderstedt,
Germany*

legal deposit June 2020

ISBN: 9782322235384

cover picture :

license: cco 1.0 universal / (cco 1.0)

graphics: Yoann MERITZA

« Open this last door »

A FEW WORDS ABOUT THE AUTHOR

Yoann MERITZA is a coach and an essay writer specializing in personal development.
He is also the author of the bestseller "How to reprogram your subconscious mind ?"

He was born on March 28, 1978 in Bonneville in Haute-Savoie and grew up in Cluses in the same department. He studied accounting and trained as an SME-SMI collaborator where he learned NLP (Neurolinguistic Programming). He has participated in numerous internships and seminars on communication and is passionate about personal development. Self-taught at heart, he continues to perfect himself in communication and the study of human nature by following in the footsteps of many authors of the same theme such as Napoleon Hill, Norman Vincent Peal, Florence Scovel Shinn or Doctor Joseph Murphy.

He creates his own method by synthesizing from his many readings on the subject and brings readers to a broad understanding of the field of personal growth by a simplified approach for assimilation at all levels, his concern being always the precision of the theme chosen and to provide novice readers with clear and affordable answers at all cultural levels.

Son of a veteran and former soldier, he is also a member of the 27ème BCA and UNC-Alpes friendship.

Introduction

Some time ago, I had an interview with a literary blog in which I was talking about my life as an author and my books.

During this exchange, I announced my plans to write a new opus the following year and that I was doing a year-long break, and somewhere, I lied to myself, because I write the one -this.

Why this decision? It was stronger than me, a sudden urge, who knows? Perhaps also the desire to share with you all that I have learned and what I still learn. During these few months in which I took a break from writing, there have been changes, life is constantly evolving and I have become a professional coach.

Some people will say to me "then! During the few years that you had written books, you weren't a coach? ", I will make the following modification to this question" I did not have the certification of coach and my books were not books of coaching, but of philosophy of life! (Understand this nuance!)

I will add this, and as a coach, I learned it during my training. It's a hint that should "tilt" in your mind. I even invite you to think about it often. We are all coaches, the only difference is that I have learned and I continue to do so, to improve myself! The rest is just a certificate giving me an authorization to exercise this function (in administrative terms).

I will give you some other clues that we are learning in the coaching profession. And these are the basics of what we are taught.

- We are still learning: What I mean by that, whether you are a novice or not, learning new techniques is an integral part of the job. We are constantly learning, and besides, I always receive training requests from private organizations. I still attend seminars, I read books on the subject, and I often watch videos, and that allows me to dig deeper on the subject.

Some will tell me that by dint of digging, I will find oil! It's a bit of an idea, but I will develop!

- A coach is never an expert in several areas: The one who claims to know everything is "the coach of nothing", and in this sense a certified coach has very few areas where he improves, and for my part, I only specialized in three areas around personal development and I continue to learn from these three areas.

- A coach always acts with humility, respect and wisdom: Especially in personal development, and understand these two words "PERSONAL DEVELOPMENT", our field is not to compete with each other by saying "you are not as good as me ! "

I open this parenthesis to make things clear, and even if some are at a more advanced stage than me in terms of coaching, you will never see a certified coach say that he is an expert in a field, that would imply that he has nothing more to learn, and on the whole, we all respect each other, novices or not. We don't have all the knowledge, but we have the basics, and this is more important than anything else to progress.

The gist of everything I just mentioned is this, we are all the coach of our own lives, and you will understand this by reading this book in its entirety. My role here is not that of mentor (I don't like that word), but rather of guide or messenger, because all that I know and all that I continue to know, you will have it now here.

To return to this book, everyone will have their own idea on the subject, I respect everyone's opinions of course. All the information you have will be brought to your attention is only that which I have at my disposal.

You will notice, by reading my books, the evolution of the information provided, it is never all, but it is always a little more.

Let's get to the point since this is what you are waiting for!

Some time ago I met someone who showed me a book called "The Spirit's Manual". No one else knows this book, it has never been published, but it contains a treasure trove of wisdom.

It is a very old manuscript and a translation of a text in Italian, it includes detailed instructions and diagrams. All I know about it is that it has been passed down from generation to generation and it would be difficult for me to give you the exact date of its creation.

I no longer have this book. It was only given to me for a few hours because, as the owner said, he should not leave his home.

Also, this book, which has only a hundred pages, is part of a collection of twelve works. Each of them has very specific instructions, and whoever holds these books would also have very great knowledge, not to say very great power.

Many people have tried to find these books that have been the subject of territory conquest for thousands of years, without success.

These books are not for everyone, and to read them you have to be very open and believe in them. I only had one copy of one of them in my hands, or rather, I had the translation of one of these books that have traveled from country to country and from generation to generation . They include many translated texts, the origins of which most probably date back to very ancient times.

Some skeptics will say "How do I know?" ", I am only transcribing the words of its owner, because unfortunately I do not have all the details, and yet, I would like to tell you more.

The originals have never been found, but there are more or less precise translations of which I do not know who currently has them.

What follows is just an interpretation of everything I have read from this book. There is a lot of information missing, some has been adapted and researched. I have read a lot of books on the subject including "The Secret" by Rhonda Byrne, and the text contains a lot of information, but which does not include all, It lacks some important elements.

I will be very brief in this manual which is intended to be as simple as possible, precise and short (I will try), I will give you just the essentials of what you need to know, but it will be up to you to work on this knowledge. Here you are the coach, you are in charge of your life.

We cross many doors, these are the ones of our evolution. They lead to success or failure when we decide to push them. We all experience this moment of hesitation when we arrive at a door allowing us to realize our dreams and what is behind remains a great mystery, and the decision is yours, and yours alone, to cross it, it s is your destiny.

Remember that you are responsible for your life, the decisions are yours, I will only make suggestions here, and it also depends on what you really want.

Last thing. Everything mentioned in this book is true. Some people will influence you by telling you not to believe me, and I will say that the only choice is yours, and that listening to them will simply demonstrate that you are still under the influence of these individuals.

There are truths that must remain hidden, I just warn you to listen to the right people and who will tell you that all decisions are yours.

I would be of the same opinion, all the decisions belong to you. The captain of your life, it's you alone!

I send you all my friendships

Yoann MERITZA
Specialized Author

I - Learning

Currently, and what I don't know is your level of involvement in your life, are you ready to change? Are you ready to change some of your beliefs? Where will you just read this book for fun and put it in a corner (unless you read only a few pages), to return wisely to your daily life?

Remember! You're the one in charge of your life, and you're the coach, I'm just passing on some information, and what you do with it will ultimately depend on YOU ONLY!

In adulthood, some people think they know everything about life. This may be your case, it has been mine for many years, long before someone kicked my butt and said, "Go ahead! " This person put me in my place. And who was this person who made me want to learn new things? Indirectly, it was myself, and beyond that, it is after many readings that I do and where I discovered that I still had a lot to learn, and this became a need for knowledge , this need to dig deeper on a subject that fascinates me, personal development.

What I especially remember from the coaching is that "Everyone is capable! " Ability does not mean being able to do everything, but to question yourself, and I do it personally, to see very often, and all because I learn new information, it is knowing how to take a step back on yourself and above all learn to listen.

You are all capable of great things, but are you sufficiently involved in your personal life to know how to question yourself when necessary?

I will give you a graphic representation of my vision of life in general and of society. Everyone has heard of the Maslow pyramid. Everyone gives their own definition of life in relation to this pyramid, but in your opinion, at what level can we be at the maximum? In society at large, we are all at "our" highest peak. I say "our" because the reality is this, the top floor of this pyramid, we never reach it, because the more we evolve in life, the more we learn.

As Jean Gabin would say, and I invite you to listen to the song "I know! Be careful at the end of this song which ends with "I know you never know, but this I know! "

The top floor of this pyramid is only reserved for a higher consciousness. It's the source. We can get it all from this source, and for that you have to be curious and involved. This "source" is unlimited.

I would say that the top floor is something virtual, and it is something that very few know. We all have access to it but subconsciously we ignore this part of our "being", or at least we misinterpret it.

According to Maslow, the top floor is self-realization, the culmination of all our dreams, which ordinary people believe is within their reach, but it only focuses on the outside of being. The top floor is reached only for those who believe in it, and for those who know how

it really works, this is our identity, our "I am!"
"

In society, we only have a watered-down vision of this "I am", the human being is made to evolve, but what very few do not say and who control this power is that everyone can have access to it, and it's even the absolute right of every human being. I would even say that those who control this power do not want you to know all the possibilities you have at your disposal, because the most dangerous weapon for them is none other than your mind, and the ability to make your own decision. , to redefine who you really are.

For years, you have been led to believe that you are incapable beings, and that you were destined for nothing other than what you had learned, making you dream and making you believe that you were "free". But what is freedom? Getting up every morning, going to work for a meager salary to pay you for leisure, and believing that you are at your highest potential and that you are destined for nothing other than what you have been taught?

The reality is that you are far from reality, one that goes far beyond your imagination. I know that many who have studied the laws of the universe like me will understand me, and even better if there are real enthusiasts on the subject.

I have been passionate about these subjects for a few years now and it has become my hobby to seek new information. I have read hundreds of books on this subject and I learn again and again and again, I will explain to you later in this book why it should be done!

You are perfecting knowledge, but you cannot know everything, neither can I! And it would be very arrogant for me to tell you! We're just tweaking it every time!

The top of the pyramid is "divine", we could equate this to God for believers, or we can give it another name "the universe". It's an unlimited source that's available to everyone for the simple reason that everyone carries part of this universe with them. We are all part of a "whole", connected by something more powerful than human consciousness. We are all part of a whole that we call "creation", of which each of us is the creator, and subconsciously we all are.

I say "unconsciously" because many people will refuse to give you access to this information, which is, however, your most absolute right. Some people will not believe me by saying this, but all the beliefs that you have (I'm not talking about religious beliefs here), are false. And you've been trained to think from childhood that you cannot get the life you want.

I read a book a few years ago, written by Dr. Wayne W. Dyer, the exact title of which I can no longer remember, which spoke of the divine source that is in each of us. According to him, imagining that this source is the ocean, and that you draw a little water from this ocean, what is in your bucket is always this ocean.

This ocean is the divine source common to each of us and from which we are born, it is the universe, everyone can have access to it, and it is your right.

IT'S YOUR RIGHT !

We are all part of a single "whole", and it is in this "all" that the origin of existence resides.

You know ? I know many people who are interested in this subject, some of whom will never tell you, or will tell you, how they got access to this informations, subject to a fairly substantial financial contribution.

Many people will probably not believe me, I understand and everyone is free to think what they want, and to stay in this environment which seems peaceful to them, this comfort zone where everything seems to be for the best, or at least, you are used to it. You have your own beliefs, it's completely legitimate, but those beliefs are only a fragment of all the possibilities that you would have easy access to. I recommend that you be very open-minded for this, because it will only be up to you to take into consideration all that I am going to tell you.

We are all stopped at self-esteem when we are at the maximum of this pyramid, and there are three categories of individuals at this level.

In the first category, there are those who master and understand all the laws of the universe, but very few will share this knowledge, unless you are a "winner". The term "winner" is something I would call "wrong" because basically we are all "winners", or at least you can have a choice. And all that I will entrust to you will depend only on you alone, because I give you this freedom, that to believe me or not, but if you are open enough, you will live with passion all your existence, and maybe even that you you will be more passionate about the subjects of philosophy, and more particularly those of the law of attraction.

There are those who aim for the top floor of this pyramid, learning constantly, over and over, and who get a little more advanced knowledge. Remember this! It is this willingness to learn that you must have constantly.

And then there are also those who think that they are at the top of this pyramid, and that they have obtained all the knowledge they need. These are the ones we meet most often on a daily basis and who often start their sentences with "I ...". "

- I did this or that, I know everything, I ... ... I, I ... ... I, I ...

What these kind of ignorant do not know, because they are ignorant in the sense that they think they know everything after having read two books of philosophy in their life, and the worst in all this is when these "philosophers" are called Desproges or Colucci.

Be careful, I'm not saying I have something against them, but take a look around! Who most often evokes Desproges or Colucci? These are the people you can meet in bars, who have very little money and who are dependent on social services (check it out for yourself!).

They believe they know everything about life, but their knowledge is really limited, it is that they very often fall back into the lower levels of this pyramid, why?

These kind of people have a need for "security" (lower level of this pyramid), they need to reassure themselves, to say that they are the best, but who have not tried anything concrete in their life. Deep down, if you remove the bark, they feel worthless and incapable, they don't feel good in their life. And they just believe that they cannot change anything in their existence.

Notice that they are the only ones who identify themselves thus, but what seems paradoxical in all this, and that they do not know, is that it is seen or understood. They are identified as narcissistic perverts in most cases.

There are those kind of people that we all meet, and who pretend to have a lot of science, those that we can meet in bars and dependent in the majority of cases on social services, they constantly ask themselves why nothing goes into their lives, and that's the problem.

They believe that .... and these beliefs are so entrenched that they cannot see life differently. They are dominated by what is called "ego", and want to feel superior, when nothing predisposes in their life to this state. Too in tune or too aware of their reality, they feel that their life cannot be otherwise, and if they really wanted to? They should be a little more open-minded, but they cannot, because it is too ingrained in them, nothing will change until they are open to other ways of thinking. The possibilities are limitless.

Are you going to make the same mistake as them and continue your peaceful little life on a meager salary until retirement, or will you seek to improve yourself again, again and again and again?

Are you going to click and start listening to others, I mean of course the right people?

How do you recognize a good person? I do not pretend to be far from it, and as I said, I am a novice in the field, but who modestly has some knowledge among the vast possibilities of the universe, and I continue on my momentum to learn more in order to retransmit it to you then, and so on.

The first good person is yourself and I have no control over your free will. Your beliefs belong to you, I have no influence on it, and you are the only one who should learn, not I who teach you. I am not your teacher, I am not your personal coach (although I have a title of coach). The very first person you should listen to is yourself! The rest is just information. The gives you the tools, it's up to you to do the repairs with.

Some will not read the book until the end, and this is a shame, although I try to shorten it, I have a lot of information to give you and to make it short is not impossible, but does not make it easier for me task.

Right now, I'm just scratching the surface of a very big topic and again asking you this question, how involved are you in what you really want? Do you want to learn or not?

Do you feel you know enough or are you prepared for the change? Basically, what is change?

This phrase has always made me smile! There she is !

"The only thing that does not change in the universe is change, the same goes for ignorance! "

You understand ? Meditate on what I have just mentioned!

Then, and this is important, beyond learning, there is training. In a chapter later in the book, I will explain why it is important to train.

Train yourself to learn again, again and again and I say this to everyone who reads this book. GET INVOLVED in what you want!

Why am I saying all this? This is important in the law of attraction process so that it turns to your advantage you will understand gradually if you are curious and passionate enough.

Some will say to me "Yet, I am curious and passionate, but nothing is happening! Why ? "

I will reply "Everything is happening!" All the time, and it depends on where you are, because not everyone evolves at the same level.

Where you are is your point of attraction. You are the nerve center of everything that is going on around you! Your environment is part of you and I will develop more and more.

You don't attract what you want, but what suits you best where you are!

Then, if you read books like the law of attraction like me, you will find that some are very good, and others are less good, how can we tell the difference when we are not used to reading them?

There are novice authors (I prefer to say "beginners" than bad). I told you, I respect everyone, even those who are new and it's a good point, why? Because they are passionate about the topics of the law of attraction and they want to build their dreams and have challenged themselves to write a book. I reassure these new writers, I was too, like everyone who has become over the years leaders in the field. In this sense, I encourage beginners to learn more, you are on the right track, and I admire you.

There are the average authors who have a little more control over the subject, but who do not yet have all the knowledge at their disposal. I never claimed to be a leader in the field and I am still learning. Everything you read is information that I have verified. These average authors are starting to make themselves known very slowly and are in the "intermediate" phase, although I am known in several countries and sold a lot of books, one of which has become a best seller, I have not still the notoriety of an author like Napoleon Hill or Norman Vincent Peal. I prefer to remain modest on the subject, even if I have a lot of answers to give you.

And of course there are the leaders, those who have the best knowledge of the subject, like those I mentioned before. They have more knowledge and have nothing more to prove. And what's also curious is that each of the leaders has a different vision of the law of attraction, I can explain!

Some would say "It's easy! "Yes, it is, but for those who understand the basics and apply them. It was "easy" for them, because they weren't on the same level as you when they started, and they have a whole different mindset. Were their old beliefs firmly entrenched or were they open to change? Were they closer to the transition path (the tipping point) between one situation and another?

What is most important is to consider "where you are!" And not everyone starts at the same level. And for some, the work may be long enough, for others, it will be quick, because it depends on "where you are!" "

I mean of course the point of attraction and why it doesn't work to your advantage, because you're on the wrong side of the equation, even if you don't recognize it right away.

Your life has been built on one and the same pattern since your childhood, which is your point of attraction. And it's up to you to determine where it is.

Why are you not passionate? Why don't you believe it? Why is nothing working to your advantage? Why aren't you as involved as you claim? Why do you have this state of mind?

I reassure everyone, nobody sucks! I would say this in these words "you have not yet mastered the basics of this law!" », And you can progress! You have the capacity, it's in you!

Everything will manifest in proportion to where you are! Do not expect to make millions if you are not prepared! How do you prepare for the best? By having better thoughts? How do you get better thoughts? My answer will surprise you, but this is the key:

By always seeing life from the good side, even if the circumstances prove the opposite! Remember regularly that behind the cloud there is always the sun.

Easier said than done would you say? that's right ! And why is it so difficult for some and easier for others?

Because you are not all on the same level. So when you have a dream and a goal, you can believe it, it will come true if you are sufficiently involved, if you believe in it, and if your state of mind turns to positivity.

The representation that I give is that of a board placed on a stone, it is called "The theory of the tipping point". It is tilted and you are located on one side of this board, with both feet on it, One side of this board (where you are!) Is negativity, and on the other, positivity. And then you go up and you feel that gravity pulls you down and makes you come back down to where you were.

And then you try again and again, but gravity always pulls you down and makes you come down, and so on, until you are used to it, your leg muscles will have developed.

And you make it hard to reach this famous tipping point where everything can change for you, it is the transition point, because after this point, everything will seem easier for you in positivity, because the slope will be descending.

You want something "unachievable", or at least in the position you are in, where your point of attraction is. For others, the point of attraction is higher on this board and are closer to the tipping point.

I'll give you an example to be clearer, imagine that you want to become a lifter and you want to lift a weight of 100 kg, you would say to me, it's impossible, and that's the problem, you don't believe it not, or at least, the current conditions of where you are do not predispose to lift this weight of 100kg, because you do not believe enough that it will one day be possible, you do not get involved enough to get there , and you do not have the necessary state of mind, because you are in tune with your environment, and nothing is in harmony with your state of mind.

But if, modestly, you start with lighter weights, 10kg or 20kg, and if you train for a long time, then you can move on to something more important. You will understand that these 100 kg are not so inaccessible as that.

You keep this goal in mind, but you will first need to go through stages.

What keeps you from believing in the law of attraction for it to work to your advantage is that you expect a result, and there is no result, just natural consequences. Nothing will appear if you don't believe it, your state of mind is not aligned and your level of involvement is at its lowest.

If your level of involvement is the same as someone lifting 10kg weights, and after a while you say to yourself "It's too tiring! I give up, I will not succeed! », Then that means that you want everything and immediately, but that the conditions for that to happen are not yet there!

Take the example of a person who is in a difficult situation. This person is constantly receiving bills and is riddled with debt, so desperate, what is their state of mind? Are the conditions favorable for him to think positively? In context, absolutely not!

But if this person believes in it enough, that he has this assurance that things will improve, that he has this flame, this very small flame in him, and if despite everything he has the feeling that everything is going to be improve, then, it will improve, BUT BE CAREFUL! This will improve to the level where it is! You will be able to reach a very high level, and before that, you will have to work on yourself.

I'm going to make a confession to you. When I was younger, I was not really passionate about studies and I often thought "it's tiring! And I was drawn to video games, friends and other outdoor hobbies.

At school we were forced to read books, but I admitted that I didn't have a great passion for reading, and my biggest excuse I found for not reading was "I don't have time ! " My level of involvement in this area was lowest, and even later, I was still in this state of mind. When I think about it, I say to myself "what a waste of time! " I started reading about ten years ago one day when "I had time! ", There was no internet connection and I had nothing planned, so I started to read a book. At first it was not very useful to me, but subconsciously, I had recorded information, and when I knew how to answer questions, I wondered where I got this knowledge from. I myself was surprised by the experience. I thought the book was insurmountable, but now I take my time to discover each author.

Currently, I read around a book every four days and I devote an hour every day to this reading. It relaxes me, it fascinates me more or less depending on the author, but I read them all.

If you read at my own pace, about an hour a day, how much would you have read in a year? And only devoting a single hour to 24 hours should be a daily ritual for you (I call it that).

Books are not a waste of time, which is not to read them! You can't pretend to be better than a proven author by selling millions of copies, most of which are best sellers, and in these books you shouldn't just see pages and cover, in these books, there is much more than that, beyond the theme or its history. In these books, there is a soul, the identity of the author, others call this "the claw", it is its deep essence, there is life in it, and it is this which allows an author to defy time and death. To perpetuate a form of existence through readers. Their soul still exists, is still there.

I understand how hard it is for you to read books, and I still wonder how you got to this page if you are not so passionate about it? If you can read this one, then you can do it for others. When you are too used to a system which consists of devoting yourself to video games, internet, facebook or others, you find time for things that are, for the most part only hobbies that will bring you nothing. concrete in the end, think about it!

Whether it's lifting a 100 kg weight, reading a book, or watching a documentary, you're not used to doing it, however, you are used to finding excuses for not doing it, while an hour a day is nothing in a day, but if you want to dedicate your life to learning nothing new, then you will end your life without having learned anything new. this is how it works. Get used to it! Train yourself !

The secret to getting rid of your old life patterns is nothing more than training! And you have to do it with the right people who have done something concrete.

I'll tell you a little story. It comes from a book by Florence Scovel Shinn entitled "The secret door to success"

Five foolish virgins and five wise virgins went to meet a great king. He had to choose a woman who would bring him an oil lamp.

In front of the kingdom gate, all had an oil lamp, but only five of them had brought oil into vases to fuel the flame.

As a result, an oil-free lamp was useless, so the ones that were chosen were the ones that carried oil. Those who had no oil stayed in front of the closed door of the kingdom because they were unprepared.

If I speak to you about this passage of a book, it is that it reflects very well what I have mentioned so far.

Many have read this book so far and I congratulate you, it shows me that you are interested in the subject and that you want to know more things, you are thirsty for knowledge, as for others who feel involved , serious, interested, passionate, who believe you are, if you are, you should be on this page, even further still, and without having skipped passages.

Do you want to turn on the light of knowledge? Very good ! Did you bring oil to fuel this flame? Having an oil lamp is fine, but it's absolutely useless without the essential ingredient, that is, the oil.

A person who is sufficiently involved in matters such as the law of attraction understands what I am talking about.

All the answers, you can have them! But applying them is something else! It is very difficult for an individual who is not used to recognizing it, so ingrained in old patterns. I'm giving you the lamp, it's up to you to add oil.

Someone who is at a very advanced level in positivity will see events always turn in their favor, whatever the circumstances.

There is no mystery, and everything you have in life, you have manifested it whether you like it or not, and it all depends on your beliefs, your degree of involvement (a fierce desire to 'go further), and your state of mind with which you will have to fight.

Train yourself ! Train yourself ! Train yourself ! And don't stop doing it!

How to proceed ?

Right now, no matter where you are, every day, train your brain to be positive, even if the circumstances are not right because they are part of your mental environment. The process is simple to put into practice, two things are enough:

- Set a goal and keep it in mind, and even better than that, think you have already achieved it without expecting any results. You will say to me "and the story of the one who wants to lift a weight of 100 kg? "

Great athletes prepare mentally, as if it were possible! It can be everyone, a coach, a business manager, a footballer, everyone in these categories is training mentally all the time.

Better than that ! Write your goal on a piece of paper and hang it on the wall in a place where you are likely to see it often! It will remind you of your goal.

Even if you are not at the optimal level, keep this goal in mind, it is "your goal", and do not wonder when it will appear, it will happen anyway.

At the point where you are, look at your surroundings and say to yourself "this will get better! "It will get better!" " For those who can't! Feel as if you have received a check for € 1,000. It's easier for the human mind to design something that is within reach.

Imagine that you know that tomorrow you will receive this sum and that you know it firmly, that everything will turn out in your favor, in all circumstances, even if the circumstances do not lend it, always direct your thoughts towards something better, and tell yourself as often as possible "everything will get better!" And be sure!

Later, I will give you all the answers you need regarding the law of attraction.

For those who want it, let's continue!

II - Boogeyman

Everyone has heard of Boogeyman who lived in the children's bedroom closet. Parents used to tell you "beware of the closet monster!" "

For the majority of us, we have been taught to be wary of what was behind the doors, and are very symbolic of what will follow over the pages. I of course want to talk about limiting beliefs.

This culture of fear when we were children gave rise to a feeling of mistrust in life events. It's a bad indicator that limits the will of sentient beings

Unconsciously, we have all become hostages of this fear, and I say it in the broadest sense of the word, because it has prevented us from exploring all fields of possibilities.

The most paradoxical in all this is that courage is born from this fear, it's two words are like beacons that we have in our mind. I'll explain why right away.

We are all born with a mind that needs benchmarks and that proceeds by labeling, what we call "symbols" or "icons". There are sensory indicators, such as touch and hearing which informs us of pain or pleasure, these are the natural barriers of our body.

If we take an everyday object, such as a pan on a stove, nothing tells us that it is hot or cold when the flame is out. We can only assume that it is in one form or another of these states with our eyes, but when we touch it, we feel pain. The organic mechanism starts.

The same goes for a sound, we can listen to soft music or a shrill cry, our body is very well formed and can alert us of danger as well as pleasure.

This constitutes our sensory symbols which depend solely on our organism. We interpret them according to our feelings.

And then there are the other symbols, those that are instilled in us, and without outside help, we can only count on our free will, I want to talk about those things that gave birth to these fears, all that we learned from those around us who told us that something was good or not good. And here I come back to the story of the closet monster.

As young children, we have all heard of Boogeyman, and for the majority of us, our parents told us that if we did not sleep, the Boogeyman would come and get us, and that he lived in the closet.

The Boogeyman is the symbol of the prohibitions of our childhood.

"Don't open this closet! "
"Don't do this or that!" "

And all this had a direct impact on our psychology, having constituted our first beliefs. And the most paradoxical in all of this is that our parents learned this from their parents and this has undoubtedly been passed on from generation to generation. All this constitutes family culture, and directly dependent on the surrounding social environment.

We've all heard phrases like

" Stop dreaming ! "

"You will not succeed! "

"It's not for people like us! "

But without these beliefs, what choices would we have made? Have we decided to open this door?

If no sensory indicator turns on, we see only a single door, and what is behind it, in reality, we do not know what is hidden there. All we do is "assume" without verifying it. They are simply predictions of what is behind it.

What is behind this door is "good" or "bad" experience, that is to say that we will have "knowledge" (the real one) and we only rely on what the parents told us . Have they been subject to a bad experience?

The bad experience only concerns one individual, the one who was exposed to it and reacted according to his feelings, and this one individual influenced all those he met. And what we don't know is if this person actually went into this closet, or if he just stopped in front and invented all kinds of stories to demonstrate his bravery to face a monster that probably does not exist not ! Who really knows what is there?

Does the Boogeyman exist or does it not exist? What is behind this door will remain a mystery until you push it "alone", and only then will you know the truth. Good or bad experience?

This door exists in your mind, it consists only of your limiting beliefs, and behind it hides a "personal" experience (good or bad).

The thing to remember from this story is to never listen to everything you are told and to trust only your gut. It's up to you to make your own choices, even if those around you are against you or trying to influence you. You are the captain of your life! isn't that my captain?

This is the only reason why you do not move forward, because you have not experienced "personally" (notice that I insist on this word) what you wanted deep inside, and it is just as important to free yourself from the barriers of your mind, the "they say" that have caused you harm, and therefore, you are in tune with a reality that may not be yours, the one that you imposed.

What you need to understand is that not everything you were told was "YOU".

Your real being is for another mission in this world and it is YOUR ONLY to find out.

III - The attraction point

Be very attentive to what I will tell you shortly! You will have a good part of the answers to your questions.

As I said, the most important thing is to determine who you are and what you really want. That said, some will likely read this book to the end, but will ignore all of the things I will cover in a very short time.

The point of attraction is where you are and especially who you are!

If you don't know "who you are?" You will not understand the basic laws of existence. " who are you ? "And more important than" who are the others? And it's only by determining who you are that you can understand who the others are. I mean you need to do your own analysis.

We are going to take the problem upside down, or at least, the way you understand it! You expect a lot from others, but in the vast majority and in reality, it is others who expect a lot from you. I say in most cases, because it is not always the case, and you will understand this soon enough.

We meet in our society two types of individuals, those which are open and those which are closed, and I do not know in which category you are exactly, and also perhaps, you do not know it yourself!

Those you meet depend on who you are, those you hang out with depend on who you are, and those who admire or criticize you depend on who you are. And everyone you've known and events in your life have only one common thread .... you alone.

Look around! What is going on ? Who are you meeting? Who are you dating? What kinds of events do you see most often? What is your perception and your state of mind?

If you want to change others, it will be a waste of time, or at least it will not be possible if you do not change yourself.

And you ? Are you ready to change? Are you prepared for change and all its consequences, because for those who correctly apply the law of attraction, they are aware that there will be changes. what are you ready to give up for that?

These changes relate exclusively to your current life, this is your point of attraction. And many do not want to give up their current life, that is to say, their old patterns, or in other words, their daily lives.

What you risk is losing friends and finding new ones. Why ? Because everything will line up with your point of attraction, and if you want change, and no one around you is prepared for it. Your state of mind will change, your beliefs will change, your level of involvement will change and they will no longer be aligned with those you hang out with.

You probably know the expression "that looks alike comes together!" "And it will be!

This is the part that the vast majority of individuals do not want to change, because they are afraid of losing everything!

If you are someone very open to these theories of the law of attraction, and no one around you is sufficiently involved in the subject, you may lose them!

This is the scariest part of this law, the fear of losing everything, but tell yourself this! You will not be able to change everyone, and probably you will be able to change a few, if they are as determined as you are to want to change.

Then you have to know what you really want, stay with people who are not ready to change, or evolve at the risk of losing everything and meet new people who are in harmony with what you are? Think about that.

Knowing who you are is also doing your own analysis! What most people do is, when they have a problem, they blame others. Why are events not turning in their favor?

Look at what you do most often, who you hang out with and what happens to you in your life, it's all connected.

In my training as a coach, there was one sentence that stayed with me.

"If your four best friends are broke, chances are you're the fifth!" "

You will only meet people who will be of the same nature as you! And if you think you can get everything out of life by including others, you are wrong, unless they are receptive to it, which I doubt very much.

Another important point! Is your mind prepared for change and all that it entails? Let me explain !

Your mind is built on patterns, and neural connections are used to what you are! And you will understand that it may take time to create new ones, and that is why I insist on starting now.

The point of training is to get your mind used to new patterns, which is not yet the case for you.

You cannot be connected to the frequency 681hz if you are only on 162hz, These frequencies cannot pass from one station to another. Your life condition will not change overnight, you will probably need a very long preparation and it will only depend on you!

If you constantly think about something you want, if your mind is not trained, it will reject it because it is not used to it, all attempts will end in failure, and the saddest thing is that you will give up in the face to these failures. It will be tiring for you! And this is where I give you a very big recommendation.

Be more interested in what you want! Get your mind used to seeing yourself in a certain situation and feel it as if it has already happened. Even if it is not yet visible, it is manifesting itself.

When you do it often, it will become more and more part of you! And also, have a passion for what you do! Let it become an obsession!

Singers, great painters, heads of state, basketball players, footballers, and even personal development coaches have all succeeded. Why ? Because they all trained with passion and determination, and that's what you don't have yet.

Get your mind used every day! Think about it all the time! Focus on what you want and life will show you that you are on the right track.

What are these signs? Pay attention to what will follow!

You will probably lose friends, others will happen for the simple reason that everything that looks alike comes together, and you will be different from those around you.

Then there is the mirror theory (or karmic laws), everything around you is similar to you, it is your point of attraction. You attract everything you think about, but also everything related to your actions, it comes back to you like a boomerang, so be careful with that!

If you want to grow in a business, but all the signs show you the opposite, rest assured! The universe answered you and offered you what is best for you! Losing a job means that there was no opportunity for advancement in this business, and that the universe brings you something better. But of course, if you misinterpret it, the negative consequences will follow.

Open up to the field of possibility! This is happening to you! Losing your partner will mean that you will find someone who suits you best based on your point of attraction.

A car that breaks down will mean that you shouldn't go where you plan to go! This is a good thing, because the events that will follow it will confirm it.

If you want to travel from New York to Daytona in the middle of the night, you know there is a long way to go, you will not see Daytona for a while. All you can see is a road lit by your lights. Everything you see with your headlights will be 30 to 100 meters from you.

Always keep the goal in mind and practice! Daytona exists, but you don't see it yet, and you will have to drive again and again! Do not be discouraged !

Your environment will correspond in every way with what you wanted. Believe me ! But be patient!

Just before closing this chapter, just a word about what is called "the present moment". Your point of attraction should always be on the "now".

There is a certain problem of interpretation concerning this "present moment", and how does one define that we are in this state?

First clue, I said "be patient!". I understand your eagerness to make everything you want in life come true, and it will happen without a doubt!

Do not anticipate and be quiet! Have a glass of water or a coffee and relax! Look forward to what you already have (in your mind), feel good and enjoy your new life (always in your mind)! No longer worry about when it will happen, what you need to know is that it is already present somewhere, regardless of why or how! What you just need to know is that it's there!

Get your mind used to it being "there"! Even if it's not visible to the human eye. It will appear in your life, but be aware that it makes you very long mental preparation first if you are not ready.

Have a fierce conviction that it is already there and imagine, feel its presence!

The mistake that many make is that they are in a hurry for results. Stop waiting for the results right away, it will always bring you back to your original situation and you will not move forward!

Rest assured that it's already there! Train yourself ! Train yourself ! Again, again and again! And when your mind is well prepared to lift a weight of 100 kg, then it will!

IV - Perception

If we are all a part of the universe, then we are the universe. We are all part of something much bigger than we could imagine. But we all have, or at least, for those who do not know it yet, a restricted perception of this universe, because we are looking for it in the wrong place.

You could identify the universe with all that is around you, and you imagine that you cannot go further, when the universe is infinite. From birth, you had identified the universe with everything around you, but what about what is in you?

If I had to make a comparison to the life you live, imagine a bird born in a cage. His environment remains this cage all his life, and he realizes that there is something much bigger, the living room where he is. His only perception comes from the information he has accumulated throughout his life, that is to say that he believed in this reality, it was, from birth, in his paradigm, and in his knowledge, there n there was only this cage and beyond that, the living room. This is part of this bird and it knows nothing else. He is not even aware of the immense power within him, that of influencing events, and one might assume that he would be able to imagine the owners or a young child setting him free. He might think of flying freely in the living room, but what he doesn't know is that the world is much bigger. A world he has never seen or even tasted the experience of being outside.

His "outside" only comes down to the living room, because he only has this information. But if he had learned of a larger universe, and he would be able to imagine another "freedom," he would be on the branch of a tree to sing.

You are like this bird and for you, life is like this cage and what you want is like the living room, that is to say that it only comes down to what you know. It goes far beyond that and you are looking for something in the wrong place.

You have a strong dominance of the outside world and you think it is limited, while it is quite the opposite, because there is a secret door that you know, but that you do not really know how to use in my best way than she is. This door is a combination of your fears, your doubts, your lies, and it was built by beliefs that you have been taught.

You have been given the image of a freedom that you do not have, and this door leads to something much more powerful than the imagination alone, a place that unites with the whole universe, it is a hidden cornucopia from which you can draw all your deepest desires, and this cornucopia is the source, a fragment of this universe much larger still, but limited by your knowledge.

It's a place where you can be whoever you want, but it only opens if we really believe in it, and if we know how it works.

The real world, the one you live in, is outside of you, but there is another world, the one of your dreams, and you cling to the idea that they will never come true and yet .....

Imagine that these dreams came from another reality, and if you believe in them firmly, they will come true.

I am sure that some people will not believe me and may not take me seriously, to those there, I would tell you to "pretend"

Florence Scovel Shinn, Rhonda Byrne, Mickael Losier, Norman Vincent Peal, Joseph Murphy and a lot of authors on the subject know what I'm talking about, and yet you take them seriously, despite the information that seems to be surreal, or because you think it is.

Each of us has this infinite source, a universe where our desires are born without ever believing that it is possible, and I can guarantee you that your dreams can take shape if you believe it! Want answers on the law of attraction? I give them to you! And in a sense, apart from a little time, what do you have to lose?

This is because your mind is too used to beliefs, or at least you have been used to that, believing that there is only one possible world, the one outside us, and you are focused only on this one, while two worlds can be in harmony from the moment you believe in it!

Everything starts from what is believed to be true and as many famous authors and men would say:

"Everything that the human mind can conceive and believe, it can do." (Napoléon Hill)

"If you can imagine it, you can create it! " (Walt Disney)

"Be the change you want to see in the world! " (Dalaï Lama)

"The greatest discovery of our generation is to realize that a man can change his life by changing his way of thinking! " (William James)

The key is to believe it! If you do not believe it, nothing will happen, even if you are not prepared for it, because despite all the information I give you, do not expect it to appear in your life the next day !

It is you alone who are the creator and the creation, you are the architect of your life, I do not ask you to take my word for it, but to have a slightly more open mind, because you are limited only to what your eyes show you, your outside eyes.

But when we firmly believe in it, and know how to use the inner eye, that of our imagination, and consider it as another possibility, then anything can happen.

Why does it take time to happen in our life? Lack of experience! You are very little used to seeing and believing in the inner eye, and it sounds like science fiction, but what keeps you from trying?

The real world is the one inside you, or at least the one inside your mind, and it can be a weapon that you can learn to use to your advantage.

This is why you have to know "who you are!" ", YOU determine the life you want to have, not others because of their beliefs that they teach you! You have the power to change everything, and it is in you, in your mind, your imagination, it is the source from which you must draw.

Imagine a cornucopia in your mind. Inside is everything you want! in a way, what you want, you already have, in this cornucopia which is nothing other than your mind, through its creativity and imagination. Suppose this world I am talking about is real (and it is for the one who truly believes in it), it is your inner refuge, a place where only you can enter.

Your desires do not come directly from the outside, and you are waiting for a result, proof that it really works, but you will never see it until it is part of you.

It already exists in your imagination, and what you need to know is only "it exists!" ", You already have what you want in your imagination, but you are not trained enough to see the experience of imagination as something real. Why want proof? It's that you doubt the existence of what you want, so if you don't believe it's already there in your imagination, it's that you don't have it!

We must believe ! Believe that you already have it, no doubt, expect a result or hope, because these are the indicators of lack! Do you need to have proof of something when you are convinced that it exists?

I'll give you a quote that I like that sums up everything I just said, and it will be up to you to meditate on it:

"The infinite is not in the vastness, but in the lowest common denominator! "

The lowest common denominator is "the universe", and if you perceive this as something big, look inside! In your imagination hides a reality that is not perceptible in the outside world. Something much bigger is the source, the origin of all lives.

When you get the object of your desire directly from your mind, and you feel that you have it, that it is in you, only in you, it will materialize in the physical world, because you are in harmony with your imagination that you perceive as "true", and from this second when you take this (the object of your desires) for granted, according to the law of attraction, if your doubts are blurred, if you firmly believe in them, as if it were real, then it is!

You have immense power, that of "now", the present moment when you are all that you can be, do or have. This immense power that arises in your mind and grows inside of you until everything you desire is realized in the physical world.

It exists in you and outside of you, and merges the imaginary and the real in a soft harmony, an infinite space.

YOU ARE THE CREATOR !!

If you follow my recommendations by following this straight path from the imaginary to the real, believing your desire to "be" (that is, "to exist"), then it is!

You are the generator that materializes your thoughts, it feeds your life with your beliefs, and the more you believe in it, the more it will light up your life.

*Infinity is not immensity
but the lowest common
denominator and it is the
source of all life!*

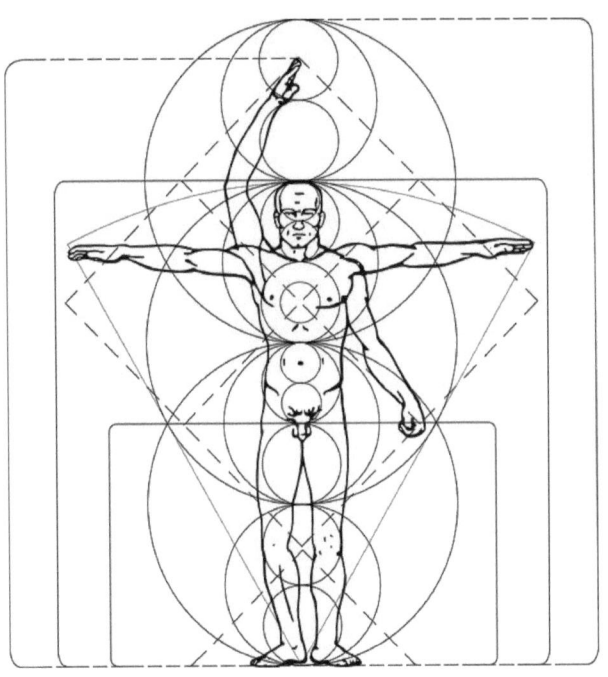

V - Training

I feel your impatience to know all the answers regarding the law of attraction, and I know them, but you will have to be attentive to what I am going to tell you.

For those who are passionate about the subjects I share, everyone has read books like "The Secret" by Rhonda Byrnes, who have applied, or at least tried to apply all that has been mentioned in this book, and for 99% of cases, it does not work! And they firmly claim that it doesn't work, why?

I myself have written books on the subject, and I have given you many answers, and as I often say, I am not a magician and nothing will appear from a magic hat.

Remember this:

The law of attraction works all the time, but you don't see it, and it only takes a few tweaks in your life for everything to turn to your advantage.

Although some have already tried to put into practice all the indications of these books (which are very good books and which I respect!), Nothing has manifested itself as they would like, and the most paradoxical is that it worked for a short while, and expect a quick protest.

It will make you smile, because everything worked! Everything you believed in, and for the most part, what you still believe is manifesting. Something that is not noticeable to the human eye.

Pay close attention to what I'm going to tell you, as this is THE real answer to your questions.

In any case, everything you think about is manifesting in good as in bad, everything continues to happen and it depends on several elements including your beliefs, your degree of involvement and your state of mind . And whenever you have a belief, a degree of involvement and a certain state of mind, it manifests itself all the time.

When is the best time to start applying all the principles of the law of attraction? I will tell you that it is up to you, but the best time is "now". The sooner you practice the techniques, the sooner it will manifest to you.

You have all the objectives more or less big, but nothing happens despite that you put months and months to practice these techniques, I give you the first reason.

The first is that you don't believe it enough. So eager to see results. But there is no result and there never will be. What you should interpret as "results" relates to St Thomas who wants to see the hands of Christ.

I'm not talking about results, but natural consequences, and it depends exclusively on everything I said above about your beliefs, your level of involvement and your state of mind.

It is not your fault, nothing is really stated in the books on this subject which give as many techniques as you want, and if you do not take into account what will follow, it will never work, you will have nice to try, but nothing will happen.

My first question will surprise you, but do you really believe it? What I mean by that is "when you tried the techniques, did you have absolute faith?" "

Many people can say they believe in it, but that's not enough! Try the techniques, practice constantly and give up after a month, six months, or a day, all because they haven't seen the results (when it was just starting to show), of course , everyone is free, but I find this sad.

Then I come to the level of involvement, are you curious enough about everything? Are you thirsty to know more? Or are you just sitting in a chair meditating, meditating, meditating until you hope it happens? After a while you give up because nothing "visible" has come up (I'll come back to that)

Finally, what is your state of mind? Are you happy ? Unhappy? Optimist or pessimist? Do your own analysis and ask yourself "who are you deep inside?" " People may pretend to be happy, but nothing around them predisposes to happiness, and this often reminds them, and condemns them to stay in this situation.

"If the truth is inside, the lie is outside! "

First you need to clearly define who you are! And to recognize that your situation is not bright, it is not very complicated.

Also, you must firmly believe in it, that is to say, have absolute faith in your desires, if you are attentive to this, you will get there!

And also to get involved as a passionate being, get more interested as I do, dig more and more, read books on the subject, listen to videos on the subject, have this thirst for discovery. This must be your first longing. Add passion, passion, enthusiasm. Easier said than done, but remember what I mentioned above, do not expect to lift a weight of 100 kg if you are not predisposed to do so.

You will implement all of this once I have explained the "why?" "

Why is nothing going in your favor and nothing showing up?

The answer is "everything manifests" depending on your beliefs, your state of mind and your level of involvement.

"Good things and bad things happen all the time, all the time," and the reason that nothing shows up to your advantage is that the law of attraction clings to the point where you are!

How far are you? In a catastrophic situation? In an average condition? In an optimal situation (these are the ones who have the best control)?

Define who you are and how you are! This is the first key.

Take a good look around and what you have! Does that make you happy? Recognize it!

Is your state of mind ascending or descending? Let me explain :

Do you think that "everything will get better" at all times (and you must always keep this state of mind in mind), or does everything you see around you give you a feeling abandonment or negativity?

Aaaah, I feel this impatience to know everything! What you need to learn to practice the law of attraction for you.

What very few books say on this subject is "determine where you are and who you are!" "

Not everyone is on the same level, and no one evolves on the same level. There will be some for whom it will be easier than for others. Why ?

Simply because you have not reached the tipping point, or at least you are further from it than others. This tipping point is when all things start to get better for you, but at the start, you shouldn't expect to see your desires materialize when you get there!

Imagine a plank on a stone and you are at one end. You start to move forward, but nothing happens! So you keep going, and nothing is happening yet. You advance more and more, and you find that it becomes more and more difficult to climb this inclined board. Then, a little before arriving at this tipping point, for a reason that only you know, you give up, when there were only a few steps left, so that you would reach this tipping point and everything would turn to your advantage.

Your level of involvement, your beliefs and your state of mind are shaken, simply because you have the impression that nothing is happening! And the reason is simple, it's because the whole weight is on the same side!

But if, despite everything, you move slowly, without running, then you will approach this famous tipping point, and you will see behind you that the board will start to rise, keeping you in balance in the middle, and as soon as you take one more step, the board will descend to the other side.

Those who got there the best were already close to this tipping point, and depending on who you are, you have more or less way to go on this board. So don't be discouraged! Everything will happen if you keep moving!

Do you understand better why it doesn't work for everyone the same? Because some are more ready than others!

Second very important point, you really have to train yourself to have positive thoughts, and I will explain how to do it.

There are many techniques for feeling good, but here I will just give you mine and each will make their own opinion.

Again, do not wait for the "results", this may discourage you, and I will tell you that the "results" are already there! You would say "how is this possible?" "

The how is not the question, and there is none to ask, it is already there, even if you do not see it!

Why can't you see it? Here is the answer !

1.61803398875

Some people are wondering what that means, and probably some people are pulling their hair out on this answer, but I will not leave the suspense lying around any longer!

It is the golden number, or otherwise called "the divine proportion" and the whole universe revolves around this number, giving it a perfect balance. It is he who gives birth to the stars, planets, plants, and animals, it is the point of origin of all life in the universe, including yours.

Everything in the universe evolves according to this number, and even in nature, everything evolves according to this rule.

The point where you are "is" your point of attraction, and each action you take according to your thoughts are related to the situation, the degree of involvement, the state of mind and the beliefs that you have!

The more you evolve from your point of attraction, constantly having positive thoughts, the more you will approach your tipping point.

And if you are aware of what is going on, everything will turn out in your favor, even if the results are not visible.

Everything in the universe will react in proportion to the point where you are in positive as in negative. Positive and negative events will be more intense or less intense, but it will depend on where you are!

For that, do not expect big results when the conditions are not favorable for that, because everything reacts in proportion, and once you clearly understand this, the small events in your life that will be positive will gradually turn into something a little bigger.

These are the rules of nature and the universe, a seed cannot become a plant in a day, because it follows a growth cycle.

When your state of mind changes, circumstances change!

Now, I'm going to tell you about your desires, everyone has them, but everyone vibrates with a great impatience to get what they want, and this is not the best way to proceed.

What you want is your goal, but you neglect what happens in proportion to where you are!

You want the big stone, but life only gives you small pebbles, but you have to understand that all this leads you on the right path.

Accept the little gifts of life and it will offer you more, and complain about what you do not have, and life will give you more in proportion!

The law of gravity follows its own rules, those of attraction too, and if your point of attraction leans more in negativity, if your thoughts are negative, you will get more in relation to the volume of negativity that you have, and conversely, if you have very little positivity, life will give you very little in proportion.

This is how the law of attraction works and not otherwise!

Then there are those for whom it worked for them, and I repeat again, it depends on where you are and it really works!

If you want physical evidence, you have all the time, but it is so tiny that you cannot see it. Just be very careful!

Keep in mind what you want as your horizon and be attentive to everything you come across on your way! There are events in your life that will turn in your favor, even if these seem to you to be the opposite!

The universe brings us the best for us according to our expectations and responds exactly to our needs, and it brings us what makes us feel good, and it works in a well-defined order and always brings you what you want for good and bad.

Your point of attraction is always evolving, and it is you who move the cursor according to the point where you are on one side or the other.

If you want something that will make you feel better, you will have it in the outside world, but you already have it in the inside world!

Don't be impatient! Especially not ! Firmly believe in the moment!

The results are always in proportion to where you are, so don't expect to receive more until you understand the signs that you are on the right track.

What you want will not appear, but will evolve. A plant also follows a cycle, it is seed before becoming roots, before the first leaves germinate.

Always be happy with what is happening to you and keep telling yourself that things are improving, and there you will have the proof that it works!

BE CONFIDENT !

Bill Gates, in an interview, gave the secret to his success, and he replied that it was having a deep vision.

What is deep vision?

If you see a seed, what do you see? Only a seed you would say to me! others will answer a plant, and others will see in it a green garden of all these similar plants. When you see beyond the seed, and what it could be, you have this vision.

THE INTERIOR ALWAYS MATCHES THE EXTERIOR! WHAT YOU WILL RECEIVE WILL NOT BE BUT IS ALREADY! LET IT JUST TIME TO TAKE LIFE!

Your goal is to have this vision in depth, without waiting and by recognizing the signs that the universe is sending you, and the more you will be grateful for this, the more the universe will send you more and in proportion to your state of mind which will evolve like a seed which becomes a plant and which becomes a green garden.

Émil Coué had created a method to always see life on the bright side.

During his sessions, he made his patients say "every day and in every way, I am getting better and better" by making them pinch the 20 knots of a cord with their fingertips.

This is exactly how we modify our point of attraction, thinking that it will get better and better, in five minutes, in an hour, in a day, and so on! You orient your internal compass on the right side, towards your goal. it is happening very slowly and gradually, the more you will believe it with the physical evidence, the more you will have. Your faith will increase as you witness events turning in your favor!

Things will always work out, believe me!

Now I give you my technique! I invite you only to try it, but be aware that it will only work from the point where you are and proportional to your state of mind, your beliefs and your degree of involvement. It will grow in you without you realizing it!

Extend your arms straight in front of you, palms facing your eyes!

Think very hard about what you want! What you want is right in front of you in the palm of each hand, and put your hands near your eyes, run your hands over the sides of your face and stop behind your face! Put your hands in front of you and do the same thing as many times as you want, saying to yourself the following thing "every second, things get better, I feel better and get closer to my goal ……. Every second , things are getting better, I feel better and I am getting closer to my goals …… .etc… .. "

what do you think is going to happen? You will have a feeling of feeling better and the more you practice, the more it will be!

To give you an image of the process, imagine that you are in the middle of the ocean, and in the distance there is an island paradise. Where you are is your point of attraction, that is, more or less far from this island.

The island is your goal, and to get there you have to swim. The more you do it, the closer you get! The more you move your arms when you see this island being closer, the more enthusiastic you feel when you say "I'm getting there!" I arrive there ! "

This is how the method works, you must have the same feeling as when you swim to reach this paradise island.

Keep in mind that tomorrow will always be better with a goal in mind and you will get closer to it, the main thing is to have your beliefs, your state of mind and your degree of involvement clearly increased.

Tomorrow, you will know the circumstances proving that you are on the right track and you will be attentive to the signs!

All of this will get in your way and you need to be grateful every time, all the time!

Last tip! Drop your eagerness and don't put a date, IT'S ALREADY IN THE OUTSIDE WORLD! Just learn a little more, train yourself to be optimistic and have a positive feeling, while firmly believing that what you want has already happened! You have control, you have power!

How else can you explain this?

Everything that happened in your life, you caused it by your thoughts and old beliefs that have accumulated throughout your life. What's going on outside is just a reflection of the inside. What you think happens directly or indirectly.

What you see all around you is in harmony with what you have accumulated throughout your life.

You must shine with new harmony as if it were part of you. If you feel that nothing fits with what is inside of you, or that you don't believe it, nothing will happen.

To be in harmony is to be one with the universe. When, for example, you want to have better health, you have to feel it as if it were already in you, that this thought is real, and that in all circumstances, even if external events show you the opposite, you must constantly perceive yourself in good health.

Do not focus on the outside! It's the answer to your thoughts, but focus on yourself! Imagine something, feel it constantly. No longer look with your eyes, do not hear with your ears, but do it with your imagination.

Hence the interest in creating an interior world, free from all external pollution, and the key to this is meditation. Make this experience a reality. Create osmosis between your thoughts and the outside world. Everything must be aligned.

The only really valid reason why nothing happens in your life is that you hold on to the roots of your life, you hold on to your past, your lived experience, your current life, what you notice, and it is essential not to no longer align with the outside world, but align with your thoughts and imagination.

It doesn't matter what happens outside LET THE UNIVERSE DO HIS WORK!

The results are not visible, or better yet, imagine that everything you want has happened. What feelings would you have? Or what feelings do you have when you are given a gift? GIVE YOURSELF THIS GIFT!

The reasons why the results are not visible are that they follow the rules of evolution of the universe. From where you are (your current situation), if your balance tilts to the negative more often than not, the power of positive attraction will be very low.

You have to give it more strength and constantly think of the positive, and let events take place.

What you focus on happens all the time, the only difference is that if you have a negative temper, you are more likely to see negative events because the pull is much stronger.

Feed your mind, your thoughts, your imagination with positive thoughts! Meditate two hours a day and then, with training, do it as often as possible.

Your imagination is a magnet that attracts everything and the power of attractiveness is much stronger on one side than on the other.

You are going to do the following thing, and from now on, you will make a firm commitment to no longer focus on external events, and by doing this, imagining all the best happening to you, even if bad events still occur in your life. life, it means that your negative attractiveness is still strong, but tell yourself to stop paying attention to what is going on negative and to feel good in all circumstances, the events positive will come to you, at a very low intensity, but they will come to you! Pay attention to this.

According to the law of divine balance and proportion, negative events will have less force, and positive events will have more force.

As curious as it may seem, the only way out of a vicious circle of bad luck and already to stop pretending that it does not work, because negative events happen. Remember this:

- What you think is always in harmony with the outside world

- What you have experienced is in harmony with the outside world

- Everything you feel is in harmony with the outside world

- All the thoughts and feelings you have accumulated result in …… ..the outside world

Something keeps you in your state, it is the importance that you give to the outside world, of which you are the creator. What is unfortunate is that the more you see your life, the more you give it importance and the more you pay your attention to this outside world, while everything is created from the inside, THE CENTER OF ATTRACTION IS YOU!

If you want a dream life, it must first exist in your mind, and you must imagine it as if it were real, feel it, rethink it, imagine that you have already lived it and that it is still in happening, without waiting for an external result, this is what ruins all your work of attraction towards positive events.

Your mind is the seed. Let it take root in you, let it grow and become a germ, then let it grow again to become a young tree, then grow again to become your tree of life.

The tree you have is that of negativity whose roots are deeply rooted in the ground, and what keeps it alive is your negativity. But always remember that if you feed this tree with your negativity, it is always in proportion to its size. Positivity is still just a tiny seed that you will feed with your positivity in proportion to its size.

I hope you understand better now! Try this technique over and over again! Increase your enthusiasm, your belief, your level of involvement and your state of mind, and everything else will follow, I promise you!

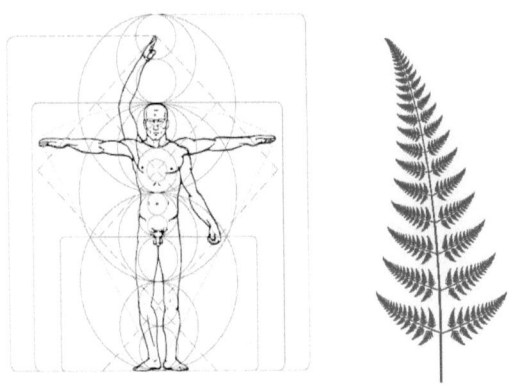

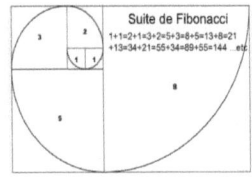

Everything in the universe depends on the same
rules of evolution in proportion to size. Little size
have a little evolution, and bigger size obtain the
bigger evolution.

It's the divine proportion

VI - The beliefs

Throughout your life, you have imagined a monster behind the closet door, or at least you have assumed, believed that there was one, and yet there could be something else entirely, the Schrolinger's cat, a trunk, or even nothing. Who knows what's behind this door? The answer is as follows! What is behind "is"! What you think you are "is"!

And in that, that's what keeps you from moving forward, that's believing, but not in a good sense Your mind is still connected to your old beliefs, so connected to them that everything that happens to you in your life has been accepted unconsciously.

We are constantly living with beliefs, good or bad, and those beliefs come to life from the moment you value them! I know I am not very clear on this.

Your beliefs are the fuel of each of our lives. Let me explain !

On all occasions, we use our beliefs which are derived from information that has been given throughout our lives. It is what gives strength or not to an event or a thing according to the intensity which one grants to him.

The door I'm talking about in this book are those of your beliefs, it's the only limit you have between your dreams and reality, between ignorance and knowledge.

There is nothing else than what you think is inside!

To give you an example, if you want to know everything about the law of attraction (and I know that the subject is very vast, and that I don't yet have all the knowledge at my disposal), if you want to practice it , but that you don't believe it from the start, it is useless to know the techniques to get there, but let me make a confession! You are subconsciously using this law of attraction. How? 'Or' What ? Simply by your beliefs.

For many years, I was interested in personal development, and more particularly in the law of attraction.

I attend many forums on the subject and many people have differing opinions, and many do not believe it because, according to them, it does not work!

Is this a problem with the interpretation of these laws? Not always !

All those who attend this kind of forum go there either out of simple curiosity, or because the subject fascinates but do not know how to apply it, and unfortunately, there are others who absolutely do not believe in it and who come to lower the morale of the group.

I often read comments

"Anyway, it doesn't work on me!" "

Because, for them, it is out of the ordinary and reacts to their beliefs, and sometimes they make fun of those who are passionate, taking this for a form of "sect".

It makes me smile, because I never pretended to be a guru, a magician or anything else, I do not sell dreams and everyone takes what they want to take, this is information that I share without problem .

Why didn't the law of attraction work the best way for many people?

These people said "I did everything right! "

I would say "NO! "

Others will say "this is it! I understood how it worked! "

there again "NO! "

The only reason the law of attraction has not worked in the best way is that it has been used in the wrong way.

Everyone will make their own opinion on the subject, I only give mine, then this is only for you!

This allowed me to identify the structure of the human mind and its different modes of operation.

Our mind is built on beliefs, as I said above, by markup "or labeling", what I mean by that, at times in our lives, we have had sensory and psychological indicators (by saying of our entourage).

Have you thought about why we all have different paths, different lives? And above all different opinions?

Are we capable of succeeding such a business? When you were younger, you felt like other people around you were better than you.

Remember that brilliant student (unless it was you), who had good grades in school, was he better than you?

When you think back to all those situations where you felt like you were either null or incapable, is it because someone told you, or did you check it out for yourself and adopt a proper interpretation of a (or) event (s)?

What if I told you that you had exactly the same chances as those that you put on a pedestal?

What is going on in our mind is made up of beliefs whether we like it or not.

We are all our own limits and it is only these that keep you from moving forward! What you believe "is"!

I will develop a little more!

Everything that happens in your mind constitutes your universe and according to your beliefs, it is always achieved by the force of your thoughts. Unconsciously, you have attracted everything that happens to you for good and for bad, and what constitutes your point of attraction is what you believe most often.

For example, if you think you are null or incapable, the circumstances of life constantly show it to you, and the more it shows it to you, the more you believe in it, and it's an endless cycle if you don't understand this basic principle .

To come back to the subject of the law of attraction, for most of those who don't believe it, they built their point of attraction on this belief, that it didn't work!

Also, because they are too results-oriented, out of the law of attraction is never the result, but the natural consequence. There is no "it should be like this!" Because give you more strength so that it is not as you would like. You have to change your mindset and say "IT IS". and that's all !

What are your beliefs built on? On the words of others, on the perception of others, and on your own perception (depending on what others think of you).

I say it according to your external gaze and not your internal gaze, because you have not yet mastered it. When you are at the point of believing that everything in your imagination "is", then "it is"!

THE ONLY BORDER BETWEEN THE IMAGINARY AND THE REAL IS FROM YOUR BELIEFS!

Now who should you believe? Is it me as a coach? Did those discourage you?

There are many people you should listen to, and if they are of the same opinion as me, the only real coach or real person that you should listen to in particular is no one other than YOU.

You are solely responsible for what you think and feel, and all that happens to you is just the natural consequence of what you think and feel. No more no less.

And who are these other people you should listen to? Those who have succeeded, those whose life smiles, business leaders, and all the other people who are at a higher level than yours!

Who should you not listen to (or not listen to anymore?), Those who hang out in bars, those who depend on social services, those who have no money and are in debt, it is above all the latter that we should no longer listen to. The best thing is to avoid them altogether, because their negativity has an impact on your state of mind.

So that you understand my point of view, go to your bank account and read the amount of it! What level are you at? Your situation "IS" your point of attraction. At least that's what your outside perception says about what you really want.

You have been so absorbed in your surroundings that now everything that happens to you is "mechanical", and you only respond to lifestyle habits. This same environment has shaped you from the start of your life.

Let's take an example :

If you were born into a middle class family, the very first environment that you saw and absorbed was this, the culture, the habits, the people you knew made you get to the point where you are ! And subconsciously, you don't admit that it can be otherwise.

Because everything that can be otherwise is "fanciful", "impracticable", and as long as you think that this is out of the possible, then it will remain impossible for you, although you have the capacity.

Your "concrete" is what's in your bank account. It's real, you see, it exists! It is part of your "BELIEFS", are you going to check every five minutes the same amount? Of course not !

If you believe in this sum, which is an integral part of your external environment, why hope for another result? And besides, why rest on the hope of what you already have?

If you put a foam ball in a box, do you want to check if something, which is already in this box, has appeared? You will not do it! You know it's there!

"YOU KNOW IT IS HERE"

(I insist on this because it is one of the keys to the law of attraction).

Your belief is "it really exists!" ", And of course, there it is!

You know your car is almost out of fuel, the natural consequence is that you will run out of gas, because you know it, you believe it! It is a real fact.

Will thinking about refueling (with your mind) help you go further? Of course not ! It's surreal and out of your reach.

All this because according to your knowledge, and from your "rational" side responding to the laws of physics, you will not hope to have a result other than that which you thought of.

Your foam ball is in a box. The natural consequence is that she is still there (unless you are a magician).

What I mean by that is that whatever you believe to be true will come to pass in one way or another. Do not see the law of attraction as an experience to conduct, nor as an expectation, but as a FACT!

What you want should be part of your internal environment, of what you think.

Here are some clues for the law of attraction to work, this is just the outline:

- We must forget the expectations, because in the meantime, there is the need, act as if you had already obtained it. This is the shortest and simplest way of the process.

- Clearly distinguishing what you want from what you don't want, the simple fact of thinking about what you don't want gives it more strength, and vice versa and just as valid.

- Stop the interior dialogues relating to what you are currently experiencing. In your mind there is a relentless harping.

- Abandon the old erroneous patterns, the plans of your current life, and no longer focus on your past, it is behind you, what matters is what you think about the present moment, you are the coach, the architect, the creator and the creation.

As long as you are attached to the results and external circumstances, nothing will happen, just think that you have already received it and just focus on it.

In my previous books, I had given the following recommendation, that of creating a virtual universe in which you evolve, a world which has nothing to do with the one you currently live.

How to proceed ?

Make a list of everything you would like to have in life, and think about these things, feel them! Detach yourself for a few moments from the "concrete" in your mind to create another "concrete", as long as you don't believe that it is, it won't work! And there is another ingredient for it to work.

The first reason that the law of attraction doesn't work on you the way you want it to, is that you give too much importance to the fact that it doesn't work the way you want it to (I know, I repeat myself) !

It is when you place more importance on a belief that it manifests in your life.

If you don't believe it, there is no point in continuing to read this book or looking for answers elsewhere on the law of attraction, it is absolutely useless if you want something to work the right way. , but don't believe it!

Beliefs are the fuel of the law of attraction, do you hope to start a car without fuel?

Do you understand the link? Beliefs, no matter what, are frequencies that you emit to the universe. Frequencies are the glue of the universe, that means that if there is no frequency, there is no universe. Human beliefs work continuously.

What you need first is to change your beliefs to make it work, and not take this as a fantasy.

If you do not take this very seriously, I advise you to give up, as this would be a complete waste of time for you!

I come back to what you call "concrete things", do you want concrete? Everything I just mentioned is concrete!

To conclude, I would tell you the following!

- Do not always believe everything that you are told!

- Do not always believe everything that is shown to you!

Your beliefs are clean, as I said from the start, you are the only captain, the coach is YOU!

BELIEVE IN YOURSELF !

As for the concrete, look around! The other word to define concrete is the word "real", and if you sound good! Is your partner not concrete? Are your children not concrete? Isn't everything you own concrete?

The only reason you don't see your life as successful is that you don't see what you already have, and that's where I come to the next chapter.

Meditate on all this and understand that the only real barrier between you and your success is your beliefs.

VII - The Mindset

In our daily life, we meet all kinds of individuals who are plagued by more or less pleasant circumstances in their life, a car that breaks down, debts, a character spouse, etc.

Look around you! There are probably people who are constantly complaining about their lives, and above all, listen to their dialogues, they often revolve around the same subjects, and also, the vision they have of life is reflected on this that they live everyday.

A badly saped person will press that they are badly saped, or a person who has no money will press that they have no money, and constantly emphasizing what they have it or not it happens in their lives.

Now make the comparison with a person for whom, everything succeeds, is it oriented towards lack? Is she often complaining? Or is she talking about the fact that she gets everything she wants and that she is always lucky? You will not see too many successful people talking about their success all the time, unless you are a coach, they have normal conversations, talk about their projects, holidays spent in certain places of the earth, their conversations have nothing extraordinary, and for the majority of those who have succeeded, they have a particularity, they remain modest.

Analyze dialogues and behaviors well, and the more you listen to people, the more you will understand the why of their situation. It's as simple as that.

People who don't have much in their life and who complain very often will do everything to get you to join their cause.

They need "existence leadership", that is to say that they will impose their point of view! DO NOT LET ANYONE SAY WHAT YOU MUST DO! What I do personally, I give you information, you take it or not! isn't that my captain?

Another important point, and I will insist on this, even if your life seems ugly and you feel disgust, I simply suggest it to you, stop complaining!

For the followers of the law of attraction, your thoughts are facts, and analyze this sentence carefully! "Your thoughts are facts! "And what happens to you in life, I would not call it" the result ", but" the natural consequence ".

Do you think you're out of luck? Then you will not be lucky!

You think you are zero, then you will always be zero!

Everything you focus on becomes reality! Do you focus on your fate or your situation? You will be more attracted to this situation.

Complaints are your points of attraction! Complain about a soup and you will often eat the same soup!

This is just as valid for what you don't have! Feel that you do not have or not enough, guess what the universe will bring you .... little or not enough!

As I told you from the start, you are the only master on board, you are the coach, and you are the captain of your life! It's up to you to select what you really want to integrate!

Many coaches much more advanced than I will say, I am just touching the surface of a large subject, and if you like me thirst for knowledge, I invite you to learn more, again, again and again, the more you will do it and subconsciously you will understand!

So what state of mind should we be in?

Already, by not pretending more importance to what happens to you bad in your life.

What you value is your point of attraction.

"Rename" (change the feeling) of what you see, hear or think!

What I do most often is that I go outside, and I look around and listen, looking for calm. I observe a lot and without judgment to feel inner peace.

Be curious about everything and enjoy!

"Think back" to what you value!

What I mean by that, don't anticipate the disaster! In any case, whether you think right or wrong, it will happen!

Life will give you signals, it's up to you to "interpret them very well"!

Do not envy and no longer be jealous!

For example, someone who owns a very nice car will give you a feeling of jealousy, of envy, but you only give a little more importance to what he has! But what do you have?

This feeling of envy or jealousy will always remind you how bad you are, that is to say "lack of it."

Do you have to reverse the situation? How? 'Or' What ?

The opposite of jealousy is "admiration", you contemplate this beautiful car, you are in awe of what it has and you say "Wow, I wish I had the same! "

Do not look at what the other has! Forget the person who owns what you want! Without asking yourself the question of "when", "how", "why", admire and appreciate!

Admire the beautiful things around you, look at nature, the environment, in fact, the trick is to "reinterpret" your universe!

When you are in awe and feel a sense of "pleasure" by looking at what is around you, then you feel good!

And that's the most important thing too, is to feel good.

After beliefs, feeling good are the very first ingredients of this law of attraction to make it work for you.

VIII - The last door

Do you want to know what's behind this closet door? Boogeman or anything else?

Wouldn't it be simpler to push this door? I can't do it for you, it's "your door". Push it and you will know what's behind! I'll explain exactly what you need to do to improve your daily life. this is the essential phase of the law of attraction.

First of all, you have to believe it enough! If you don't believe it or have doubts, nothing will work the way you want it to.

Then you have to know how to see, listen and speak less. You have two eyes, two ears and a mouth, and they work in proportion to see twice as much, hear twice as much, and speak once as little.

Realize that if we have something to gain, then we also have something to lose! What are you ready to lose? Friends ? A relationship ?

Situations? And also know that "WHO" you will be in harmony with your environment. It will be different, and you're not used to that yet! You are not used to it, or at least your mind is not used to seeing things differently.

What I suggest to you, after having in your possession a lot of information on the subject, is to never stop learning, to train, to persevere! Get more and more interested! Be curious about everything!

What I do every day are rituals that have become a habit for me. I read often, I watch many documentaries on the internet, I learn to be more and more interested (even if I am very much, otherwise, I would not make this book!). The universe has a lot to offer us, good as well as bad, and you have to see the good circumstances in the bad, because they will always bring us something better for us.

Practice (force yourself) to read an hour a day! Force your mind to see the positive in the negative, force it to accept the reality you want, getting used to it often, often, often! If you don't, your mind will reject it, and your will will go down, be stronger than your mind and be determined.

Work on your posture and try to always have a straight body! By changing your posture and looking as far as you can in front of you, it changes your mindset. It is a physiognomic phenomenon.

Learn "who are you?" Because knowing "who are you?" will determine "who you will be?" "

To conclude this book, which is nothing more than a guide to life, if you apply all that I have just mentioned, I can guarantee you that changes will occur in your life, and it will be you to interpret them well!

On these last words, I thank you all for your attention, and I wish you all the success you deserve!

Friendly yours

Yoann MERITZA
Specialist author

SUGGESTED READINGS

ÉDITIONS BOD

- *THE LEAD OF LIFE*
Yoann MERITZA

- *HOW TO REPROGRAMM YOUR*
SUBCONSCIOUS MIND ?
Yoann MERITZA

UN MONDE DIFFERENT

- *MAXIMUM SUCCESS*
Max PICCININI

- *UNLIMITED CONFIDENCE*
Franck NICOLAS

- *LAW OF ATTRACTION*
Michael J. LOSIER

- *THE SECRET*

Rhonda BYRNE

EDITIONS BELIVEAU

- 7 ESSENTIAL INGREDIENTS TO MASTER THE LAW OF ATTRACTION
Jack CANFIELD - Mark Victor HANSEN - Jeanna GABELLINI - Eva GREGORY

POCHE MARABOUT

- THE COUÉ METHOD
Emile COUE

- THE POWER OF POSITIVE THINKING
Norman Vincent PEAL

MACRO EDITIONS

- YOU ARE BORN RICH
Bob PROCTOR

EDITIONS FIRST

- *THE LITTLE BOOK OF THE LAW OF* ATTRACTION
Slavica BOGDANOV

EDITIONS DU TRESOR CACHE

- *SECRETS OF A MILLIONARY MIND*
T Harv EKER

J'AI LU

- *THE SECRET CODE OF YOUR DESTINY*
James HILMAN

- *COMPLETE YOUR DESTINY*
Wayne W. DYER

- *WHEN WE WANT WE CAN !*
Normann Vincent PEAL

- *HOW TO SUCCEED YOUR LIFE?*
Dr Josephe MURPHY

*- HOW TO USE THE POWER OF YOUR
SUBCONSCIOUS MIND ?
Dr Joseph MURPHY*

*- THE POWER OF WILL
Paul-Clément JAGOT*

*- THE GAME OF LIFE
Florence Scovel SHINN*

*- YOUR WORD IS A MAGIC WAND
Florence Scovel SHINN*

*- THINK ABOUT AND BECOME RICH
Napoleon HILL*

*- THE SECRETS OF COMMUNICATION
Richard BANDLER & John GRINDER*

*- BECOME A MENTALIST
Bastien BRICOUT*

LE LIVRE DE POCHE

- HOW TO MAKE FRIENDS
Dale CARNEGIE

- HOW TO SPEAK IN PUBLIC
Dale CARNEGIE

EDITIONS ASKA

- SMARTER THAN THE DEVIL
Napoleon HILL

- EDITIONS « POUR LES NULS »

- THE LAW OF ATTRACTION FOR DUMPS
Slavica BOGDANOV

EDITIONS ADA

- THE SECRETS OF SUCCESS
Sandra Anne TAYLOR

- ATTRACT WHAT YOU WISH
Mélodie FLETCHER

EDITIONS BUSSIERE

- THE SECRET DOOR LEADING TO
SUCCESS
Florence Scovel SHINN